VACCINES FOR SMARTYPANTS

Anushka Ravishankar
Illustrations by Pia Alizé Hazarika

duckbill

An imprint of Penguin Random

DUCKBILL BOOKS

USA | Canada | UK | Ireland | Australia
New Zealand | India | South Africa | China | Singapore

Duckbill Books is part of the Penguin Random House group of companies
whose addresses can be found at global.penguinrandomhouse.com

Published by Penguin Random House India Pvt. Ltd
4th Floor, Capital Tower 1, MG Road,
Gurugram 122 002, Haryana, India

Penguin
Random House
India

First published in Duckbill Books by
Penguin Random House India 2023

Text copyright © Anushka Ravishankar 2023
Illustrations copyright © Pia Alizé Hazarika 2023

ISBN 9780143461036

Typeset in ArcherPro by DiTech Publishing Services Pvt. Ltd
Printed at Thomson Press India Ltd, New Delhi

www.penguin.co.in

A **VACCINE** is a biological preparation that is used to stimulate the body's immune response against diseases.

Germs are tiny living things which are inside us and all around us.

YOU CAN'T SEE THEM.

I KNOW YOU HAVE SHARP EYES, BUT THEY ARE VERY, VERY SMALL.

NO, NOT EVEN WITH A MAGNIFYING GLASS.

Some germs are good, but some germs are not. When these 'bad' germs enter a person's body, the person becomes sick.

The body fights the germs with the help of the **immune system**.

It is the immune system that comes to know when a bad germ enters the body.

Then it makes an **antibody** to attack the germ.

NO! AN ANTIBODY IS NOT LIKE A GUN!
NO, IT ISN'T LIKE A SWORD!
OR A FIST!

Each antibody can attack only one type of germ. So the immune system has to first know which germ has entered the body, and then make the antibody for that germ.

NO, THE GERM DOES NOT TELL THE IMMUNE SYSTEM ITS NAME. BECAUSE IT CANNOT TALK.
Hello germ. Who are you?

There are things called **T cells**, whose job it is to find out what kind of germ has entered the body.

Once the immune system knows what germ it is, it can make the antibody that can attack that germ.

So for each new kind of germ, the immune system has to make a new antibody.

YES, YOU USE THE SAME CLAWS TO FIGHT THE NEXT-DOOR CAT AND THE DOG DOWNSTAIRS.
BUT YOU'RE NOT AN ANTIBODY AND THEY'RE NOT GERMS.
THEY MAKE YOU SICK?
WE ARE NOT TALKING ABOUT THAT KIND OF SICK.

If the body takes too long to find out which germ it is, then the person can fall very sick.

So it's important for the T cells to quickly find out what germ has come into the body.

Once the body makes the antibody
for one kind of germ, it remembers
that germ.

So the next time, when the same germ
comes into the body, it can quickly
make the same antibody and
stop the disease.

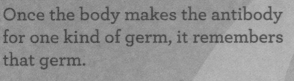

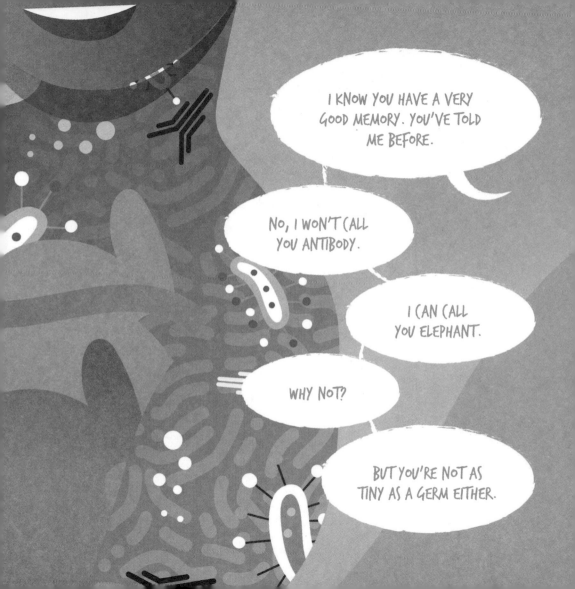

The body is ready for the germs it knows, but when a new germ enters the body, the body does not have an antibody for it.

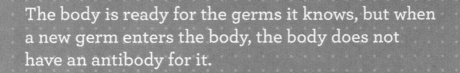

There is a way to teach a person's T cells to recognize a germ quickly, even if it has not attacked their body before.

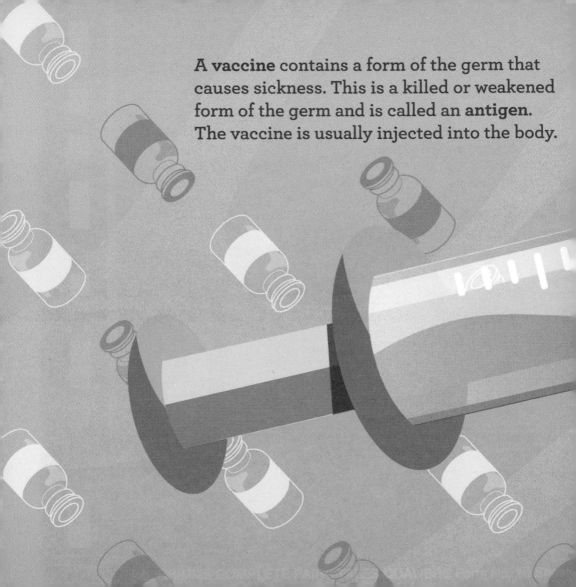

A **vaccine** contains a form of the germ that causes sickness. This is a killed or weakened form of the germ and is called an **antigen**. The vaccine is usually injected into the body.

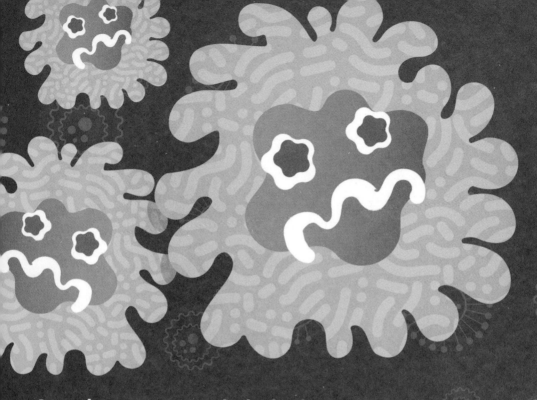

Once the vaccine is in the body, the T cells find out the antigen and the immune system makes a new antibody to attack the germ.

DON'T BE SILLY.
YES, I'M SURE!
IT'S A VERY SMALL PART OF THE GERM, TOO WEAK TO MAKE YOU SICK.

Sometimes the vaccine has to be given more than once, so that the antibody is stronger and lasts longer. This also makes sure the immune system does not forget the germ.

UMM, YES, YOU NEED TO GET THE NEXT ONE IN A FEW MONTHS.
NO POINT HIDING.
JUST BECAUSE YOU HAVE A GOOD MEMORY, DOESN'T MEAN YOUR IMMUNE SYSTEM HAS A GOOD MEMORY.

Once the body has been given the vaccine, the immune system remembers the weak germ that was in the vaccine.

So if the real germ actually attacks, it quickly makes the antibody for that germ, and gets rid of it.

That's how a vaccine protects us from the germ that it is made up of.

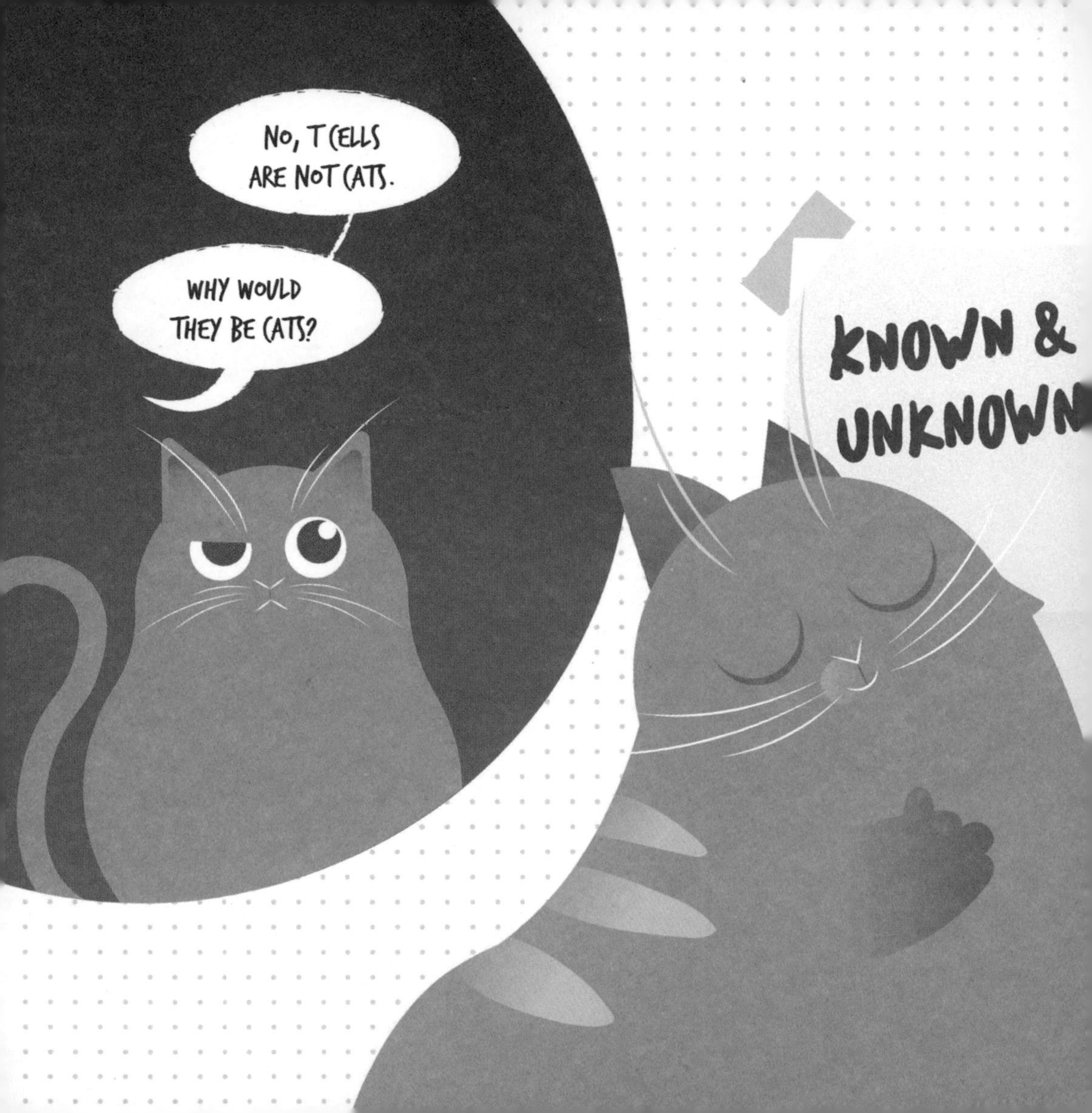

KNOWN & UNKNOWN

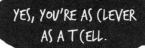

MILKMAN	PAPERWALA	COURIER GUY 1ST VISIT	COURIER GUY 2ND VISIT
KNOWN	KNOWN	UNKNOWN	KNOWN

Anushka Ravishankar likes science, cats and books, not necessarily in that order. So she decided to write a book to explain science to a cat. The cat doesn't always get the point, but she hopes her readers will.

Pia Alizé Hazarika is an illustrator primarily interested in comics and visual narratives.

Her independent/collaborative work has been published by Penguin Random House India (*The PAO Anthology*), Comix India, Manta Ray Comics, The Pulpocracy, Captain Bijli Comics, Yoda Press, Zubaan Books and the Khoj Artists Collective. She runs PIG Studio, an illustration-driven space, based out of New Delhi.

Her handle on Instagram is @_PigStudio_

Read more in the series